Our Wedding Journal

_____

and

_____

CONTENTS

Congratulations—you're getting married! Once the excitement of getting engaged has abated (just a little), you'll realize that there's a lot to organize before you can send out your wedding invitations. First of all, check out the Inspiration section of this journal. It will prompt you to think about some big decisions (from the ring to the honeymoon). You may also find a theme emerging from your responses that will influence the overall style of your wedding: if you have favorite colors or flowers already in mind, it's helpful to coordinate them now before you decide on your stationery, the cake, and so on.

The Planning section is where all your key information will be stored. From keeping a budget to finding a venue, it will help you keep track of all the necessary organizing. A comprehensive checklist, in chronological order from the engagement to the week before the wedding, will alert you to all that needs to be done. Squared pages are included for your reception seating plans.

Once you've sent your wedding invitations, the responses will come flying in. Keep a log of the replies in the Guests section. You can also note the gifts you received, thank-yous sent, and other important information here.

Peruse The Big Day chapter earlier than the night before. It's your essential reference to who does what on the day, and when. After the dust has settled on your celebrations, you can store mementoes here, and record special moments from the day. You'll finish up with a completed journal to keep and treasure.

RINGS

The classic engagement ring is a diamond solitaire, its popularity having much to do with the sparkle created by this type of cut (known as round or brilliant). Other beautiful stones to consider include sapphires, rubies, emeralds, and amethysts. As well as new rings, you could look at antique ones, or commission a jeweler to design and make a ring specially for you. Think also about the metal you'd like the stones set in (18-carat gold and platinum are very popular).

IDEAS FOR OUR RINGS

COLOR SCHEMES

Color is an easy way to give your wedding a sense of continuity. Any shade of white is an excellent foil for other colors. Choose one accent shade for a simple but stylish look, and use it for details such as ribbon around the bouquets and the icing on the cake. Gold or silver adds richness and sparkle. You could choose a single pastel: baby blue, ice-cream pink, lemon yellow, mint green, or lilac. A touch of a dark shade such as rich pink adds drama. A single color also looks good used in a variety of shades. Pink is the obvious choice, since many traditional wedding flowers—roses, carnations, lilies, peonies—come in glorious shades of it, from pale to deep.

COLOR-SCHEME IDEAS

Lemon yellow and hyacinth blue, or sunflower yellow with baby blue.

Deep pink and mint green, or powder pink with forest green.

Sugared-almond pastels—pale pink, blue, green, yellow, lilac.

Pale mauve and soft lime green.

Soft yellow, orange, apricot, and russet (an autumnal scheme).

Ruby red, gold, and forest green (rich, wintry colors).

Rich pinks and rose reds (but use deep shades with care).

Silver and pale blue or lilac.

Rose pink and gold.

OUR SHORTLIST OF COLOR SCHEMES

FLOWERS

A wedding somehow isn't a wedding without flowers. They add beauty, color, and scent as nothing else can.

OUR SHORTLIST OF FLOWER IDEAS

_____
_____
_____
_____
_____
_____
_____
_____
_____
_____
_____
_____
_____
_____
_____
_____
_____
_____
_____
_____
_____
_____
_____
_____
_____
_____
_____

THE LANGUAGE OF FLOWERS—A FEW WEDDING FAVORITES

Alstroemeria: Friendship

Baby's breath: Fruitful marriage

Carnation: The bonds of love

Chrysanthemum: Joy, long life, truth

Dahlia: Forever yours

Freesia: Innocence

Holly: Domestic happiness

Honeysuckle: The bonds of love

Hyacinth: Constancy

Ivy: Wedded love

Lavender: Devotion

Lemon blossom: Fidelity in love

Lily: Majesty

Pansy: You occupy my thoughts

Peony: Happy marriage

Phlox: United hearts

Rose: Love

Veronica: Fidelity

Violet: Faithfulness

White clover: I promise

THE DRESS

Buying a beautiful dress that will only be worn once is a grand gesture unique to weddings, and it's a big moment for any bride. And though "wedding" and "gown" seem to go together, your dream outfit may be a satin coat or a cocktail dress. Make sure it's something you feel comfortable and confident in.

IDEAS FOR HER DRESS

THE GROOM'S OUTFIT

Most grooms rent their formalwear, though many rental places sell off ex-rental clothes at good prices. Morning dress can be worn before noon, especially for formal weddings. After noon, most grooms opt for a tuxedo. A less formal choice is a suit, from cream linen for summer to navy or dark gray for winter.

IDEAS FOR HIS OUTFIT

ATTENDANTS' OUTFITS

The maid of honor or chief bridesmaid is the bride's right-hand woman, and she may be joined by other bridesmaids. For them, a good idea is to choose sophisticated dresses that can be worn again. The best man and male ushers should dress similarly to the groom. Flower girls and ring bearers add great charm to a wedding. Little girls look charming in any pretty dress, while smart trousers and a shirt or even miniature morning dress are good options for boys.

IDEAS FOR THE ATTENDANTS' OUTFITS

OUR SHORTLIST OF CLOTHING IDEAS

FOR HER:

DRESS
_____

_____

VEIL
_____

HEADDRESS OR TIARA
_____

SHOES
_____

BAG
_____

LINGERIE
_____

JEWELRY
_____

OTHER ACCESSORIES (E.G. GLOVES)
_____

GOING-AWAY OUTFIT
_____

FOR HIM:

SUIT/WAISTCOAT
_____

_____

TIE
_____

HAT
_____

SHOES
_____

CUFFLINKS
_____

GOING-AWAY OUTFIT
_____

FOR THE ATTENDANTS:

DRESSES FOR FLOWER GIRLS/BRIDESMAIDS
_____

_____

HEADDRESSES FOR FLOWER GIRLS/BRIDESMAIDS
_____

SUITS FOR PAGEBOYS/RING BEARERS
_____

_____

FORMALWEAR FOR GROOMSMEN/USHERS
_____

SHOES
_____

FAVORS

What will you delight your wedding guests with? Whatever your taste and budget, there are favors to suit: delectable cakes, cookies, chocolates, and candies; dainty napkins and handkerchiefs; romantic flowers; scented delights; magical candles; beautiful bags; and special keepsakes.

OUR SHORTLIST OF FAVOR IDEAS

_____
_____
_____
_____
_____
_____
_____
_____
_____
_____
_____
_____
_____
_____
_____
_____
_____
_____
_____
_____
_____
_____

FOOD AND DRINK

A sit-down, three-course meal is the most traditional and formal option.
A buffet gives guests lots of choice and should be cheaper. When you're
choosing a caterer, ask for edible samples. Champagne is the traditional
wedding drink, but it's expensive, so you could reserve it for the toasts only.
It's usual to serve red and white wine with a seated meal or buffet.

FOOD AND DRINK REQUIREMENTS FOR THE WEDDING DAY

CAKES

Traditionally, cake-cutting follows the speeches, when everyone's eyes are on the couple. Some couples have two cakes—a bride's cake and a groom's cake—which gives guests a choice, too.

OUR SHORTLIST OF CAKES

_____
_____
_____
_____
_____
_____
_____
_____
_____
_____
_____
_____
_____
_____
_____
_____
_____
_____
_____
_____
_____

MUSIC

Music creates a special atmosphere at a wedding. You may want to have music before your ceremony, for the entrance of the bride, and for the exit of the bride and groom, and a band or DJ for guests to dance to at the reception. If you want to impress your guests when you take to the dancefloor for the first time, you might want to take a few lessons.

OUR SHORTLIST OF MUSIC AND FIRST DANCE IDEAS

HONEYMOON

Once it's all over, you finally have a chance to spend some precious time together. When you book your first-night hotel, let them know you'll be newlyweds, as they may offer complimentary champagne, flowers, or chocolates. If you're traveling overseas, remember that the names on your ticket and passport must tally.

OUR SHORTLIST OF HONEYMOON DESTINATIONS

COUNTDOWN TO THE WEDDING CHECKLIST

once you're engaged

★ Set a date for the wedding. You may want to put an announcement in the newspaper.

★ Set your budget and decide what your priorities are. Discuss who will organize and pay for what, and make sure everyone is clear about what has been decided.

★ Arrange ahead for the ceremony—church, city hall, register office, or other location—and have a meeting with the person who will officiate.

★ Book your reception venue and caterer (remember to put everything in writing), and discuss food and drink.

★ Book musicians for ceremony or reception.

★ Draw up a guest list in consultation with both sets of parents.

★ Order wedding stationery.

★ Book a photographer and videographer (if you're marrying in church, make sure you're allowed to photograph or film inside).

★ Arrange your wedding transportation. You may need cars from the wedding to the reception and for going away.

★ Order your cake.

★ Choose bridesmaids, flower girls, best man, ushers, and ring bearer.

★ Start looking at wedding dresses and accessories, and outfits for your attendants. (It can take several months for a dress to be made.)

★ Order your flowers.

★ Start to plan your honeymoon. If you're going in high season, reserve as early as possible.

★ Investigate local accommodations for guests who are traveling long distances. Reserve rooms in good time and inform guests of this when you send out your invitations.

three months before

* Register for wedding gifts.

* Buy your wedding rings.

* Run through the form of the wedding service. Choose your music and text (for a church ceremony, discuss with your minister; for a civil wedding, check with the authorities).

* Choose going-away clothes, if you're having them. (On the day, someone will need to make sure your clothes are taken home once you've left.)

* Arrange to rent formalwear for the male members of the wedding party.

* Make sure your honeymoon plans are finalized and that you've organized visas, inoculations, travel insurance, and foreign currency if necessary.

* Send invitations out at least six weeks before the day (eight is safer). As replies come in, make a list of who is coming. Remember to send an invitation to the groom's parents. It's also courteous to invite the person who will be officiating.

* Buy gifts for your helpers on the day, such as bridesmaids, best man, ushers, and both your mothers.

* Think about taking out wedding insurance.

* If you are changing your name on your passport, send it off in plenty of time. Others to inform include your employer, bank, insurance company, the Internal Revenue Services or Inland Revenue, the Department of Social Security, and your doctor.

* Have a trial run of your makeup. See your hairdresser to try styles and book your appointment for the day.

* Book your first-night hotel.

one month before

* Give your ushers instructions for the day. It might be useful to provide brief written notes.
* Check that the best man knows what his duties for the day are.
* Confirm all arrangements for the reception, catering, entertainment, transportation, and so on and check the final number of guests.
* Make a seating plan for a sit-down dinner.
* As presents arrive, write thank-you letters.
* Have your final fittings for your dress if necessary, and try on the whole outfit, with underwear and accessories, before the day.
* Arrange bachelorette and bachelor (hen and stag) parties.
* Arrange the wedding rehearsal and the rehearsal dinner, if you are having one.

one week before

* Make final confirmations with your reception hall and caterer, photographer, florist, cake maker, and so on, and with your travel agent or tour operator. Make sure that anyone who needs it has a contact number for you, and that they know exactly where to deliver goods.
* Pack for your honeymoon. Ask the best man to make sure that your luggage is put in your going-away car or is sent ahead to your hotel.
* Wear your wedding shoes around the house so they'll be comfortable on the day.
* Have a final try-on of your wedding clothes.
* Remind the best man to return rented formalwear after the wedding.
* Try to have the rehearsal and rehearsal dinner the night before the wedding so your out-of-town guests can get to know each other and renew old acquaintances.

BUDGET CHECKLIST

                                                    ESTIMATED COST

ANNOUNCEMENTS

INVITATIONS, ENVELOPES, AND POSTAGE

PROGRAMS/ORDERS OF SERVICE

OTHER STATIONERY (PLACECARDS, MENUS, AND SO ON)

                                                    TOTAL

DRESS

HEADDRESS

VEIL

JEWELRY

LINGERIE

SHOES AND HOSIERY

OTHER ACCESSORIES

HAIR AND MAKEUP

                                                    TOTAL

MEN'S FORMALWEAR RENTAL

ACCESSORIES: TIES, CUFF LINKS, VESTS

ATTENDANTS' OUTFITS, IF YOU ARE PAYING FOR THEM

                                                    TOTAL

BRIDE'S BOUQUET

BRIDESMAIDS' BOUQUETS

BOUTONNIERES/BUTTONHOLES AND CORSAGES

FLOWERS FOR THE CHURCH OR VENUE

FLOWERS FOR THE RECEPTION

                                                    TOTAL

PHOTOGRAPHER _____

VIDEOGRAPHER _____

                                        TOTAL _____

CHURCH FEES _____

CIVIL CEREMONY FEES _____

MUSIC FOR THE CEREMONY _____

                                        TOTAL _____

RECEPTION VENUE _____

FOOD _____

DRINK _____

CAKE _____

ENTERTAINMENT _____

TRANSPORTATION _____

RICE BAGS _____

INSURANCE _____

                                        TOTAL _____

GIFTS: ATTENDANTS _____

            BEST MAN _____

            USHERS _____

            MOTHERS _____

                                        TOTAL _____

FIRST-NIGHT HOTEL _____

HONEYMOON _____

                                        TOTAL _____

                                GRAND TOTAL _____

BUDGET NOTES

_____
_____
_____
_____
_____
_____
_____
_____
_____
_____
_____
_____
_____
_____
_____
_____
_____
_____

VENUES

Make notes here about the wedding and reception venues you have considered.

VENUE _____

NOTES _____

_____

_____

_____

VENUE _____

NOTES _____

_____

_____

_____

VENUE _____

NOTES _____

_____

_____

_____

VENUE _____

NOTES _____

_____

_____

_____

VENUE

NOTES

VENUE

NOTES

VENUE

NOTES

VENUE

NOTES

STATIONERY CHECKLIST

invitations Enclose maps and accommodations information if necessary.
If you're having an evening party to which you're inviting extra guests,
there should be a separate invitation for this.

reply cards You don't have to include preprinted reply cards with your
invitations, though they may encourage your guests to reply more promptly.

thank-yous Since your guests have gone to the trouble of buying you a gift,
you should take the trouble of handwriting a personal thank-you. Try to tackle
them as presents arrive.

programs/orders of service Couples often print these for church weddings and
blessings. Inside, details of the music and text, the order of the service, and the
hymns, are printed to make it easy for everyone to follow. Establish what form
of service you're having with your minister before you contact the printer.

placecards If you're having a seating plan at your reception, you'll need placecards of some sort for the tables. They can be printed or handwritten.

menus These are optional. You could have a small menu for each guest that they can take away as a memento, or a larger one for each table. Your caterer may be able to supply them, so ask before you order printed ones.

table plans You'll need one of these if you're having a seated meal, well displayed so all your guests can easily see where to go.

table stationery You may want to go the whole hog and order coasters, napkins, napkin rings, matchbooks, and so on with your names or initials and the date of your wedding.

guest book To make a wedding keepsake, provide a book for your guests to sign. Place it in a prominent position at the reception or ask one of your ushers to circulate it.

USE THIS PAGE TO DRAFT YOUR WEDDING STATIONERY

PLAN OTHER EVENTS, SUCH AS YOUR ENGAGEMENT PARTY, REHEARSAL
DINNER, AND SO ON, HERE

FLOWER PLANNER

BRIDE'S BOUQUET
_____
_____
_____
_____

BOUQUETS FOR THE BRIDESMAIDS
_____
_____
_____

CORSAGES FOR THE MOTHERS
_____
_____
_____

BOUTONNIERES (BUTTONHOLES):
GROOM _____
BEST MAN _____
FATHERS _____
USHERS _____
_____
_____

ARRANGEMENTS FOR THE CEREMONY
_____
_____
_____
_____

ARRANGEMENTS FOR THE RECEPTION
_____
_____
_____
_____
_____

SEATING PLANS

For a formal meal, a seating plan is a mandatory idea since it avoids a chaotic scramble for places. Give yourself plenty of time to draw it up—it can be a bit of a game of musical chairs trying to get it right. A traditional top table seating plan is shown below.

Facing the table:

chief bridesmaid	groom's father	bride's mother	groom	bride	bride's father	groom's mother	best man

MAKE SEATING PLANS FOR YOUR WEDDING RECEPTION HERE

MAKE SEATING PLANS FOR YOUR WEDDING RECEPTION HERE

MAKE SEATING PLANS FOR YOUR WEDDING RECEPTION HERE

MAKE SEATING PLANS FOR YOUR WEDDING RECEPTION HERE

MAKE SEATING PLANS FOR YOUR WEDDING RECEPTION HERE

MAKE SEATING PLANS FOR YOUR WEDDING RECEPTION HERE

THE GIFT LIST

With stores full of so much desirable homeware, it can be hard to know where to begin when you're registering. Start by considering the number of your guests—don't put so many items on it that you're unlikely to get full sets of anything, and cover a broad price range so that no one feels they've got to spend more than they can afford.

OUR GIFT REGISTRY DETAILS

PACKING LIST FOR OUR HONEYMOON

_____

_____

_____

_____

_____

_____

_____

_____

_____

_____

_____

_____

_____

_____

_____

_____

_____

GUESTS

ADDRESS

RSVP   NO. IN PARTY

SPECIAL DIETARY REQUIREMENTS

GIFT

THANK-YOU SENT

GUESTS

ADDRESS

RSVP   NO. IN PARTY

SPECIAL DIETARY REQUIREMENTS

GIFT

THANK-YOU SENT

GUESTS

ADDRESS

RSVP   NO. IN PARTY

SPECIAL DIETARY REQUIREMENTS

GIFT

THANK-YOU SENT

GUESTS

ADDRESS

RSVP   NO. IN PARTY

SPECIAL DIETARY REQUIREMENTS

GIFT

THANK-YOU SENT

GUESTS

ADDRESS

RSVP   NO. IN PARTY

SPECIAL DIETARY REQUIREMENTS

GIFT

THANK-YOU SENT

GUESTS

ADDRESS

RSVP   NO. IN PARTY

SPECIAL DIETARY REQUIREMENTS

GIFT

THANK-YOU SENT

GUESTS

ADDRESS

RSVP   NO. IN PARTY

SPECIAL DIETARY REQUIREMENTS

GIFT

THANK-YOU SENT

GUESTS

ADDRESS

RSVP   NO. IN PARTY

SPECIAL DIETARY REQUIREMENTS

GIFT

THANK-YOU SENT

GUESTS

ADDRESS

RSVP   NO. IN PARTY

SPECIAL DIETARY REQUIREMENTS

GIFT

THANK-YOU SENT

GUESTS

ADDRESS

RSVP   NO. IN PARTY

SPECIAL DIETARY REQUIREMENTS

GIFT

THANK-YOU SENT

GUESTS

ADDRESS

RSVP   NO. IN PARTY

SPECIAL DIETARY REQUIREMENTS

GIFT

THANK-YOU SENT

GUESTS

ADDRESS

RSVP   NO. IN PARTY

SPECIAL DIETARY REQUIREMENTS

GIFT

THANK-YOU SENT

GUESTS

ADDRESS

RSVP   NO. IN PARTY

SPECIAL DIETARY REQUIREMENTS

GIFT

THANK-YOU SENT

GUESTS

ADDRESS

RSVP   NO. IN PARTY

SPECIAL DIETARY REQUIREMENTS

GIFT

THANK-YOU SENT

GUESTS

ADDRESS

RSVP   NO. IN PARTY

SPECIAL DIETARY REQUIREMENTS

GIFT

THANK-YOU SENT

GUESTS

ADDRESS

RSVP   NO. IN PARTY

SPECIAL DIETARY REQUIREMENTS

GIFT

THANK-YOU SENT

GUESTS

ADDRESS

RSVP   NO. IN PARTY

SPECIAL DIETARY REQUIREMENTS

GIFT

THANK-YOU SENT

GUESTS

ADDRESS

RSVP   NO. IN PARTY

SPECIAL DIETARY REQUIREMENTS

GIFT

THANK-YOU SENT

GUESTS

ADDRESS

RSVP   NO. IN PARTY

SPECIAL DIETARY REQUIREMENTS

GIFT

THANK-YOU SENT

GUESTS

ADDRESS

RSVP   NO. IN PARTY

SPECIAL DIETARY REQUIREMENTS

GIFT

THANK-YOU SENT

GUESTS

ADDRESS

RSVP   NO. IN PARTY

SPECIAL DIETARY REQUIREMENTS

GIFT

THANK-YOU SENT

GUESTS

ADDRESS

RSVP   NO. IN PARTY

SPECIAL DIETARY REQUIREMENTS

GIFT

THANK-YOU SENT

GUESTS

ADDRESS

RSVP   NO. IN PARTY

SPECIAL DIETARY REQUIREMENTS

GIFT

THANK-YOU SENT

GUESTS

ADDRESS

RSVP   NO. IN PARTY

SPECIAL DIETARY REQUIREMENTS

GIFT

THANK-YOU SENT

GUESTS

ADDRESS

RSVP   NO. IN PARTY

SPECIAL DIETARY REQUIREMENTS

GIFT

THANK-YOU SENT

GUESTS

ADDRESS

RSVP   NO. IN PARTY

SPECIAL DIETARY REQUIREMENTS

GIFT

THANK-YOU SENT

GUESTS

ADDRESS

RSVP   NO. IN PARTY

SPECIAL DIETARY REQUIREMENTS

GIFT

THANK-YOU SENT

GUESTS

ADDRESS

RSVP   NO. IN PARTY

SPECIAL DIETARY REQUIREMENTS

GIFT

THANK-YOU SENT

GUESTS

ADDRESS

RSVP   NO. IN PARTY

SPECIAL DIETARY REQUIREMENTS

GIFT

THANK-YOU SENT

GUESTS

ADDRESS

RSVP   NO. IN PARTY

SPECIAL DIETARY REQUIREMENTS

GIFT

THANK-YOU SENT

GUESTS

ADDRESS

RSVP   NO. IN PARTY

SPECIAL DIETARY REQUIREMENTS

GIFT

THANK-YOU SENT

GUESTS

ADDRESS

RSVP   NO. IN PARTY

SPECIAL DIETARY REQUIREMENTS

GIFT

THANK-YOU SENT

GUESTS

ADDRESS

RSVP   NO. IN PARTY

SPECIAL DIETARY REQUIREMENTS

GIFT

THANK-YOU SENT

GUESTS

ADDRESS

RSVP   NO. IN PARTY

SPECIAL DIETARY REQUIREMENTS

GIFT

THANK-YOU SENT

GUESTS

ADDRESS

RSVP   NO. IN PARTY

SPECIAL DIETARY REQUIREMENTS

GIFT

THANK-YOU SENT

GUESTS

ADDRESS

RSVP   NO. IN PARTY

SPECIAL DIETARY REQUIREMENTS

GIFT

THANK-YOU SENT

GUESTS

ADDRESS

RSVP   NO. IN PARTY

SPECIAL DIETARY REQUIREMENTS

GIFT

THANK-YOU SENT

GUESTS

ADDRESS

RSVP   NO. IN PARTY

SPECIAL DIETARY REQUIREMENTS

GIFT

THANK-YOU SENT

GUESTS

ADDRESS

RSVP   NO. IN PARTY

SPECIAL DIETARY REQUIREMENTS

GIFT

THANK-YOU SENT

GUESTS

ADDRESS

RSVP   NO. IN PARTY

SPECIAL DIETARY REQUIREMENTS

GIFT

THANK-YOU SENT

GUESTS

ADDRESS

RSVP   NO. IN PARTY

SPECIAL DIETARY REQUIREMENTS

GIFT

THANK-YOU SENT

GUESTS

ADDRESS

RSVP   NO. IN PARTY

SPECIAL DIETARY REQUIREMENTS

GIFT

THANK-YOU SENT

GUESTS

ADDRESS

RSVP   NO. IN PARTY

SPECIAL DIETARY REQUIREMENTS

GIFT

THANK-YOU SENT

GUESTS

ADDRESS

RSVP   NO. IN PARTY

SPECIAL DIETARY REQUIREMENTS

GIFT

THANK-YOU SENT

GUESTS

ADDRESS

RSVP   NO. IN PARTY

SPECIAL DIETARY REQUIREMENTS

GIFT

THANK-YOU SENT

GUESTS

ADDRESS

RSVP   NO. IN PARTY

SPECIAL DIETARY REQUIREMENTS

GIFT

THANK-YOU SENT

GUESTS

ADDRESS

RSVP   NO. IN PARTY

SPECIAL DIETARY REQUIREMENTS

GIFT

THANK-YOU SENT

GUESTS

ADDRESS

RSVP   NO. IN PARTY

SPECIAL DIETARY REQUIREMENTS

GIFT

THANK-YOU SENT

GUESTS

ADDRESS

RSVP   NO. IN PARTY

SPECIAL DIETARY REQUIREMENTS

GIFT

THANK-YOU SENT

GUESTS

ADDRESS

RSVP   NO. IN PARTY

SPECIAL DIETARY REQUIREMENTS

GIFT

THANK-YOU SENT

GUESTS

ADDRESS

RSVP   NO. IN PARTY

SPECIAL DIETARY REQUIREMENTS

GIFT

THANK-YOU SENT

GUESTS

ADDRESS

RSVP   NO. IN PARTY

SPECIAL DIETARY REQUIREMENTS

GIFT

THANK-YOU SENT

GUESTS

ADDRESS

RSVP   NO. IN PARTY

SPECIAL DIETARY REQUIREMENTS

GIFT

THANK-YOU SENT

GUESTS

ADDRESS

RSVP   NO. IN PARTY

SPECIAL DIETARY REQUIREMENTS

GIFT

THANK-YOU SENT

GUESTS

ADDRESS

RSVP   NO. IN PARTY

SPECIAL DIETARY REQUIREMENTS

GIFT

THANK-YOU SENT

GUESTS

ADDRESS

RSVP   NO. IN PARTY

SPECIAL DIETARY REQUIREMENTS

GIFT

THANK-YOU SENT

GUESTS

ADDRESS

RSVP   NO. IN PARTY

SPECIAL DIETARY REQUIREMENTS

GIFT

THANK-YOU SENT

GUESTS

ADDRESS

RSVP   NO. IN PARTY

SPECIAL DIETARY REQUIREMENTS

GIFT

THANK-YOU SENT

GUESTS

ADDRESS

RSVP   NO. IN PARTY

SPECIAL DIETARY REQUIREMENTS

GIFT

THANK-YOU SENT

GUESTS

ADDRESS

RSVP   NO. IN PARTY

SPECIAL DIETARY REQUIREMENTS

GIFT

THANK-YOU SENT

GUESTS

ADDRESS

RSVP   NO. IN PARTY

SPECIAL DIETARY REQUIREMENTS

GIFT

THANK-YOU SENT

GUESTS

ADDRESS

RSVP   NO. IN PARTY

SPECIAL DIETARY REQUIREMENTS

GIFT

THANK-YOU SENT

GUESTS

ADDRESS

RSVP   NO. IN PARTY

SPECIAL DIETARY REQUIREMENTS

GIFT

THANK-YOU SENT

GUESTS

ADDRESS

RSVP   NO. IN PARTY

SPECIAL DIETARY REQUIREMENTS

GIFT

THANK-YOU SENT

GUESTS

ADDRESS

RSVP   NO. IN PARTY

SPECIAL DIETARY REQUIREMENTS

GIFT

THANK-YOU SENT

GUESTS

ADDRESS

RSVP   NO. IN PARTY

SPECIAL DIETARY REQUIREMENTS

GIFT

THANK-YOU SENT

GUESTS _____

ADDRESS _____

RSVP _____ NO. IN PARTY _____

SPECIAL DIETARY REQUIREMENTS _____

GIFT _____

THANK-YOU SENT _____

GUESTS _____

ADDRESS _____

RSVP _____ NO. IN PARTY _____

SPECIAL DIETARY REQUIREMENTS _____

GIFT _____

THANK-YOU SENT _____

GUESTS _____

ADDRESS _____

RSVP _____ NO. IN PARTY _____

SPECIAL DIETARY REQUIREMENTS _____

GIFT _____

THANK-YOU SENT _____

GUESTS _____

ADDRESS _____

RSVP _____ NO. IN PARTY _____

SPECIAL DIETARY REQUIREMENTS _____

GIFT _____

THANK-YOU SENT _____

GUESTS _____

ADDRESS _____

RSVP _____ NO. IN PARTY _____

SPECIAL DIETARY REQUIREMENTS _____

GIFT _____

THANK-YOU SENT _____

GUESTS _____

ADDRESS _____

RSVP _____ NO. IN PARTY _____

SPECIAL DIETARY REQUIREMENTS _____

GIFT _____

THANK-YOU SENT _____

GUESTS

ADDRESS

RSVP   NO. IN PARTY

SPECIAL DIETARY REQUIREMENTS

GIFT

THANK-YOU SENT

GUESTS

ADDRESS

RSVP   NO. IN PARTY

SPECIAL DIETARY REQUIREMENTS

GIFT

THANK-YOU SENT

GUESTS

ADDRESS

RSVP   NO. IN PARTY

SPECIAL DIETARY REQUIREMENTS

GIFT

THANK-YOU SENT

GUESTS

ADDRESS

RSVP   NO. IN PARTY

SPECIAL DIETARY REQUIREMENTS

GIFT

THANK-YOU SENT

GUESTS

ADDRESS

RSVP   NO. IN PARTY

SPECIAL DIETARY REQUIREMENTS

GIFT

THANK-YOU SENT

GUESTS

ADDRESS

RSVP   NO. IN PARTY

SPECIAL DIETARY REQUIREMENTS

GIFT

THANK-YOU SENT

GUESTS

ADDRESS

RSVP   NO. IN PARTY

SPECIAL DIETARY REQUIREMENTS

GIFT

THANK-YOU SENT

GUESTS

ADDRESS

RSVP   NO. IN PARTY

SPECIAL DIETARY REQUIREMENTS

GIFT

THANK-YOU SENT

GUESTS

ADDRESS

RSVP   NO. IN PARTY

SPECIAL DIETARY REQUIREMENTS

GIFT

THANK-YOU SENT

GUESTS

ADDRESS

RSVP   NO. IN PARTY

SPECIAL DIETARY REQUIREMENTS

GIFT

THANK-YOU SENT

GUESTS

ADDRESS

RSVP   NO. IN PARTY

SPECIAL DIETARY REQUIREMENTS

GIFT

THANK-YOU SENT

GUESTS

ADDRESS

RSVP   NO. IN PARTY

SPECIAL DIETARY REQUIREMENTS

GIFT

THANK-YOU SENT

GUESTS

ADDRESS

RSVP   NO. IN PARTY

SPECIAL DIETARY REQUIREMENTS

GIFT

THANK-YOU SENT

GUESTS

ADDRESS

RSVP   NO. IN PARTY

SPECIAL DIETARY REQUIREMENTS

GIFT

THANK-YOU SENT

GUESTS

ADDRESS

RSVP   NO. IN PARTY

SPECIAL DIETARY REQUIREMENTS

GIFT

THANK-YOU SENT

GUESTS

ADDRESS

RSVP   NO. IN PARTY

SPECIAL DIETARY REQUIREMENTS

GIFT

THANK-YOU SENT

GUESTS

ADDRESS

RSVP   NO. IN PARTY

SPECIAL DIETARY REQUIREMENTS

GIFT

THANK-YOU SENT

GUESTS

ADDRESS

RSVP   NO. IN PARTY

SPECIAL DIETARY REQUIREMENTS

GIFT

THANK-YOU SENT

GUESTS

ADDRESS

RSVP   NO. IN PARTY

SPECIAL DIETARY REQUIREMENTS

GIFT

THANK-YOU SENT

GUESTS

ADDRESS

RSVP   NO. IN PARTY

SPECIAL DIETARY REQUIREMENTS

GIFT

THANK-YOU SENT

GUESTS

ADDRESS

RSVP   NO. IN PARTY

SPECIAL DIETARY REQUIREMENTS

GIFT

THANK-YOU SENT

GUESTS

ADDRESS

RSVP   NO. IN PARTY

SPECIAL DIETARY REQUIREMENTS

GIFT

THANK-YOU SENT

GUESTS

ADDRESS

RSVP   NO. IN PARTY
SPECIAL DIETARY REQUIREMENTS

GIFT
THANK-YOU SENT

GUESTS

ADDRESS

RSVP   NO. IN PARTY
SPECIAL DIETARY REQUIREMENTS

GIFT
THANK-YOU SENT

GUESTS

ADDRESS

RSVP   NO. IN PARTY
SPECIAL DIETARY REQUIREMENTS

GIFT
THANK-YOU SENT

GUESTS

ADDRESS

RSVP   NO. IN PARTY
SPECIAL DIETARY REQUIREMENTS

GIFT
THANK-YOU SENT

GUESTS

ADDRESS

RSVP   NO. IN PARTY
SPECIAL DIETARY REQUIREMENTS

GIFT
THANK-YOU SENT

GUESTS

ADDRESS

RSVP   NO. IN PARTY
SPECIAL DIETARY REQUIREMENTS

GIFT
THANK-YOU SENT

GUESTS

ADDRESS

RSVP   NO. IN PARTY

SPECIAL DIETARY REQUIREMENTS

GIFT

THANK-YOU SENT

GUESTS

ADDRESS

RSVP   NO. IN PARTY

SPECIAL DIETARY REQUIREMENTS

GIFT

THANK-YOU SENT

GUESTS

ADDRESS

RSVP   NO. IN PARTY

SPECIAL DIETARY REQUIREMENTS

GIFT

THANK-YOU SENT

GUESTS

ADDRESS

RSVP   NO. IN PARTY

SPECIAL DIETARY REQUIREMENTS

GIFT

THANK-YOU SENT

GUESTS

ADDRESS

RSVP   NO. IN PARTY

SPECIAL DIETARY REQUIREMENTS

GIFT

THANK-YOU SENT

GUESTS

ADDRESS

RSVP   NO. IN PARTY

SPECIAL DIETARY REQUIREMENTS

GIFT

THANK-YOU SENT

GUESTS

ADDRESS

RSVP   NO. IN PARTY

SPECIAL DIETARY REQUIREMENTS

GIFT

THANK-YOU SENT

GUESTS

ADDRESS

RSVP   NO. IN PARTY

SPECIAL DIETARY REQUIREMENTS

GIFT

THANK-YOU SENT

GUESTS

ADDRESS

RSVP   NO. IN PARTY

SPECIAL DIETARY REQUIREMENTS

GIFT

THANK-YOU SENT

GUESTS

ADDRESS

RSVP   NO. IN PARTY

SPECIAL DIETARY REQUIREMENTS

GIFT

THANK-YOU SENT

GUESTS

ADDRESS

RSVP   NO. IN PARTY

SPECIAL DIETARY REQUIREMENTS

GIFT

THANK-YOU SENT

GUESTS

ADDRESS

RSVP   NO. IN PARTY

SPECIAL DIETARY REQUIREMENTS

GIFT

THANK-YOU SENT

GUESTS

ADDRESS

RSVP   NO. IN PARTY

SPECIAL DIETARY REQUIREMENTS

GIFT

THANK-YOU SENT

GUESTS

ADDRESS

RSVP   NO. IN PARTY

SPECIAL DIETARY REQUIREMENTS

GIFT

THANK-YOU SENT

GUESTS

ADDRESS

RSVP   NO. IN PARTY

SPECIAL DIETARY REQUIREMENTS

GIFT

THANK-YOU SENT

GUESTS

ADDRESS

RSVP   NO. IN PARTY

SPECIAL DIETARY REQUIREMENTS

GIFT

THANK-YOU SENT

GUESTS

ADDRESS

RSVP   NO. IN PARTY

SPECIAL DIETARY REQUIREMENTS

GIFT

THANK-YOU SENT

GUESTS

ADDRESS

RSVP   NO. IN PARTY

SPECIAL DIETARY REQUIREMENTS

GIFT

THANK-YOU SENT

GUESTS

ADDRESS

RSVP   NO. IN PARTY

SPECIAL DIETARY REQUIREMENTS

GIFT

THANK-YOU SENT

GUESTS

ADDRESS

RSVP   NO. IN PARTY

SPECIAL DIETARY REQUIREMENTS

GIFT

THANK-YOU SENT

GUESTS

ADDRESS

RSVP   NO. IN PARTY

SPECIAL DIETARY REQUIREMENTS

GIFT

THANK-YOU SENT

GUESTS

ADDRESS

RSVP   NO. IN PARTY

SPECIAL DIETARY REQUIREMENTS

GIFT

THANK-YOU SENT

GUESTS

_____

ADDRESS

_____

_____

RSVP   NO. IN PARTY

SPECIAL DIETARY REQUIREMENTS

_____

GIFT

THANK-YOU SENT

GUESTS

_____

ADDRESS

_____

_____

RSVP   NO. IN PARTY

SPECIAL DIETARY REQUIREMENTS

_____

GIFT

THANK-YOU SENT

GUESTS

_____

ADDRESS

_____

_____

RSVP   NO. IN PARTY

SPECIAL DIETARY REQUIREMENTS

_____

GIFT

THANK-YOU SENT

GUESTS

_____

ADDRESS

_____

_____

RSVP   NO. IN PARTY

SPECIAL DIETARY REQUIREMENTS

_____

GIFT

THANK-YOU SENT

GUESTS

ADDRESS

RSVP   NO. IN PARTY

SPECIAL DIETARY REQUIREMENTS

GIFT

THANK-YOU SENT

GUESTS

ADDRESS

RSVP   NO. IN PARTY

SPECIAL DIETARY REQUIREMENTS

GIFT

THANK-YOU SENT

GUESTS

ADDRESS

RSVP   NO. IN PARTY

SPECIAL DIETARY REQUIREMENTS

GIFT

THANK-YOU SENT

GUESTS

ADDRESS

RSVP   NO. IN PARTY

SPECIAL DIETARY REQUIREMENTS

GIFT

THANK-YOU SENT

GUESTS

ADDRESS

RSVP   NO. IN PARTY

SPECIAL DIETARY REQUIREMENTS

GIFT

THANK-YOU SENT

GUESTS

ADDRESS

RSVP   NO. IN PARTY

SPECIAL DIETARY REQUIREMENTS

GIFT

THANK-YOU SENT

GUESTS

ADDRESS

RSVP   NO. IN PARTY
SPECIAL DIETARY REQUIREMENTS

GIFT
THANK-YOU SENT

GUESTS

ADDRESS

RSVP   NO. IN PARTY
SPECIAL DIETARY REQUIREMENTS

GIFT
THANK-YOU SENT

GUESTS

ADDRESS

RSVP   NO. IN PARTY
SPECIAL DIETARY REQUIREMENTS

GIFT
THANK-YOU SENT

GUESTS

ADDRESS

RSVP   NO. IN PARTY
SPECIAL DIETARY REQUIREMENTS

GIFT
THANK-YOU SENT

GUESTS

ADDRESS

RSVP   NO. IN PARTY
SPECIAL DIETARY REQUIREMENTS

GIFT
THANK-YOU SENT

GUESTS

ADDRESS

RSVP   NO. IN PARTY
SPECIAL DIETARY REQUIREMENTS

GIFT
THANK-YOU SENT

GUESTS _____

ADDRESS _____
_____

RSVP _____ NO. IN PARTY
SPECIAL DIETARY REQUIREMENTS _____
_____

GIFT _____
THANK-YOU SENT _____

GUESTS _____

ADDRESS _____
_____

RSVP _____ NO. IN PARTY
SPECIAL DIETARY REQUIREMENTS _____
_____

GIFT _____
THANK-YOU SENT _____

GUESTS _____

ADDRESS _____
_____

RSVP _____ NO. IN PARTY
SPECIAL DIETARY REQUIREMENTS _____
_____

GIFT _____
THANK-YOU SENT _____

GUESTS _____

ADDRESS _____
_____

RSVP _____ NO. IN PARTY
SPECIAL DIETARY REQUIREMENTS _____
_____

GIFT _____
THANK-YOU SENT _____

GUESTS _____

ADDRESS _____

_____

RSVP _____ NO. IN PARTY ____

SPECIAL DIETARY REQUIREMENTS _____

_____

GIFT _____

THANK-YOU SENT _____

GUESTS _____

ADDRESS _____

_____

RSVP _____ NO. IN PARTY ____

SPECIAL DIETARY REQUIREMENTS _____

_____

GIFT _____

THANK-YOU SENT _____

GUESTS _____

ADDRESS _____

_____

RSVP _____ NO. IN PARTY ____

SPECIAL DIETARY REQUIREMENTS _____

_____

GIFT _____

THANK-YOU SENT _____

GUESTS _____

ADDRESS _____

_____

RSVP _____ NO. IN PARTY ____

SPECIAL DIETARY REQUIREMENTS _____

_____

GIFT _____

THANK-YOU SENT _____

GUESTS _____

ADDRESS _____

_____

RSVP _____ NO. IN PARTY ____

SPECIAL DIETARY REQUIREMENTS _____

_____

GIFT _____

THANK-YOU SENT _____

GUESTS _____

ADDRESS _____

_____

RSVP _____ NO. IN PARTY ____

SPECIAL DIETARY REQUIREMENTS _____

_____

GIFT _____

THANK-YOU SENT _____

GUESTS

ADDRESS

RSVP   NO. IN PARTY

SPECIAL DIETARY REQUIREMENTS

GIFT

THANK-YOU SENT

GUESTS

ADDRESS

RSVP   NO. IN PARTY

SPECIAL DIETARY REQUIREMENTS

GIFT

THANK-YOU SENT

GUESTS

ADDRESS

RSVP   NO. IN PARTY

SPECIAL DIETARY REQUIREMENTS

GIFT

THANK-YOU SENT

GUESTS

ADDRESS

RSVP   NO. IN PARTY

SPECIAL DIETARY REQUIREMENTS

GIFT

THANK-YOU SENT

GUESTS

ADDRESS

RSVP   NO. IN PARTY

SPECIAL DIETARY REQUIREMENTS

GIFT

THANK-YOU SENT

GUESTS

ADDRESS

RSVP   NO. IN PARTY

SPECIAL DIETARY REQUIREMENTS

GIFT

THANK-YOU SENT

GUESTS

ADDRESS

RSVP   NO. IN PARTY

SPECIAL DIETARY REQUIREMENTS

GIFT

THANK-YOU SENT

GUESTS

ADDRESS

RSVP   NO. IN PARTY

SPECIAL DIETARY REQUIREMENTS

GIFT

THANK-YOU SENT

GUESTS

ADDRESS

RSVP   NO. IN PARTY

SPECIAL DIETARY REQUIREMENTS

GIFT

THANK-YOU SENT

GUESTS

ADDRESS

RSVP   NO. IN PARTY

SPECIAL DIETARY REQUIREMENTS

GIFT

THANK-YOU SENT

GUESTS

ADDRESS

RSVP   NO. IN PARTY

SPECIAL DIETARY REQUIREMENTS

GIFT

THANK-YOU SENT

GUESTS

ADDRESS

RSVP   NO. IN PARTY

SPECIAL DIETARY REQUIREMENTS

GIFT

THANK-YOU SENT

GUESTS

ADDRESS

RSVP   NO. IN PARTY

SPECIAL DIETARY REQUIREMENTS

GIFT

THANK-YOU SENT

GUESTS

ADDRESS

RSVP   NO. IN PARTY

SPECIAL DIETARY REQUIREMENTS

GIFT

THANK-YOU SENT

GUESTS

ADDRESS

RSVP   NO. IN PARTY

SPECIAL DIETARY REQUIREMENTS

GIFT

THANK-YOU SENT

GUESTS

ADDRESS

RSVP   NO. IN PARTY

SPECIAL DIETARY REQUIREMENTS

GIFT

THANK-YOU SENT

GUESTS

ADDRESS

RSVP   NO. IN PARTY

SPECIAL DIETARY REQUIREMENTS

GIFT

THANK-YOU SENT

GUESTS

ADDRESS

RSVP   NO. IN PARTY

SPECIAL DIETARY REQUIREMENTS

GIFT

THANK-YOU SENT

GUESTS

ADDRESS

RSVP   NO. IN PARTY

SPECIAL DIETARY REQUIREMENTS

GIFT

THANK-YOU SENT

GUESTS

ADDRESS

RSVP   NO. IN PARTY

SPECIAL DIETARY REQUIREMENTS

GIFT

THANK-YOU SENT

GUESTS

ADDRESS

RSVP   NO. IN PARTY

SPECIAL DIETARY REQUIREMENTS

GIFT

THANK-YOU SENT

GUESTS

ADDRESS

RSVP   NO. IN PARTY

SPECIAL DIETARY REQUIREMENTS

GIFT

THANK-YOU SENT

GUESTS

ADDRESS

RSVP   NO. IN PARTY

SPECIAL DIETARY REQUIREMENTS

GIFT

THANK-YOU SENT

GUESTS

ADDRESS

RSVP   NO. IN PARTY

SPECIAL DIETARY REQUIREMENTS

GIFT

THANK-YOU SENT

GUESTS _____

ADDRESS _____
_____

RSVP _____ NO. IN PARTY _____

SPECIAL DIETARY REQUIREMENTS _____
_____

GIFT _____

THANK-YOU SENT _____

GUESTS _____

ADDRESS _____
_____

RSVP _____ NO. IN PARTY _____

SPECIAL DIETARY REQUIREMENTS _____
_____

GIFT _____

THANK-YOU SENT _____

GUESTS _____

ADDRESS _____
_____

RSVP _____ NO. IN PARTY _____

SPECIAL DIETARY REQUIREMENTS _____
_____

GIFT _____

THANK-YOU SENT _____

GUESTS _____

ADDRESS _____
_____

RSVP _____ NO. IN PARTY _____

SPECIAL DIETARY REQUIREMENTS _____
_____

GIFT _____

THANK-YOU SENT _____

GUESTS

ADDRESS

RSVP   NO. IN PARTY
SPECIAL DIETARY REQUIREMENTS

GIFT
THANK-YOU SENT

GUESTS

ADDRESS

RSVP   NO. IN PARTY
SPECIAL DIETARY REQUIREMENTS

GIFT
THANK-YOU SENT

GUESTS

ADDRESS

RSVP   NO. IN PARTY
SPECIAL DIETARY REQUIREMENTS

GIFT
THANK-YOU SENT

GUESTS

ADDRESS

RSVP   NO. IN PARTY
SPECIAL DIETARY REQUIREMENTS

GIFT
THANK-YOU SENT

GUESTS

ADDRESS

RSVP   NO. IN PARTY
SPECIAL DIETARY REQUIREMENTS

GIFT
THANK-YOU SENT

GUESTS

ADDRESS

RSVP   NO. IN PARTY
SPECIAL DIETARY REQUIREMENTS

GIFT
THANK-YOU SENT

WHAT EVERYONE DOES ON THE DAY

the maid of honor or chief bridesmaid

* Helps the bride get ready before the wedding.
* Makes sure the bride's honeymoon luggage is sent to the reception or hotel.
* Waits for the bride to arrive at the ceremony and keeps an eye on young attendants.
* Arranges the bride's veil and train before she walks up the aisle.
* Takes the bride's bouquet when she gets to the top of the aisle. She returns the bouquet to the bride for the walk back up the aisle.
* Looks after the bride's dress once she's changed into her going-away outfit.

the ushers

* Arrive at the wedding well before the ceremony, to hand out program sheets or orders of service as guests arrive, and to show them to their seats.
* Escort the bride's mother and groom's parents to their seats at the front of the church (if there is a chief usher, he or she should do this).
* Tell guests where to park, and have umbrellas on hand if it's raining.

* Are ready to seat latecomers.
* Help get guests together for formal photographs.
* Help the best man organize rides for guests to the reception, if necessary.
* Make sure everyone has found their seats at the reception.

the best man

* Helps organize outfits for himself, the groom, and the ushers and makes sure they're picked up.
* Helps the groom to get ready on the day and makes sure he arrives for the ceremony in good time.
* Coordinates the ushers and makes sure they know what their duties are.
* Checks that the boutonnières (buttonholes) arrive and that the programs (orders of service) are ready to be handed out.
* Makes sure the groom's going-away clothes are at the reception venue.
* Makes sure that any fees (such as organist and choir) payable on the day are settled.
* Looks after the ring(s) and hands them to the officiant or groom during the ceremony.
* Helps to get guests together for photographs.
* Makes sure the ushers organize rides to the reception for anyone who needs them.
* Escorts the bride and groom to their car to go to the reception, and escorts the bridesmaids to the reception.
* Announces the speeches and the cake cutting (if there is no master of ceremonies).
* Reads out cards or messages at the reception, and makes the final toast.
* Looks after the groom's clothes once he's changed, and ensures rented items are returned.
* Announces the bride and groom's departure from the reception and makes sure their luggage has been packed or sent on to their hotel.

WEDDING DAY CHECKLIST

On the day, don't leave yourselves with any jobs to do. Instead, give someone
else (or several helpers) the responsibility of receiving the bouquets and
boutonnieres, seeing that any programs are ready to be given out, that the
cake has been delivered, and so on. Concentrate on getting ready. Make sure
you both have some time alone before the wedding to gather your thoughts.
Take a conscious decision to enjoy every minute of your wedding—it goes
all too quickly. Opposite, list everything that needs to be done on the day,
and the person who'll do it.

WEDDING DAY TIMETABLE

8AM

9

10

11

12PM

1

2

3

4

5

6

7

8

9

10

11

MIDNIGHT

CONTACT DETAILS OF WEDDING DAY HELPERS

SUPPLIER

PHONE NUMBER

SUPPLIER

PHONE NUMBER

SUPPLIER

PHONE NUMBER

SUPPLIER

PHONE NUMBER

SUPPLIER

PHONE NUMBER

SUPPLIER

PHONE NUMBER

SUPPLIER

PHONE NUMBER

SUPPLIER

PHONE NUMBER

SUPPLIER

PHONE NUMBER

SUPPLIER

PHONE NUMBER

SPEECHES WERE MADE BY...

TOASTS WERE PROPOSED BY...

USE THIS PAGE TO WRITE SPECIAL THINGS SAID AT THE RECEPTION

ATTACH PROGRAM/ORDER

OF SERVICE HERE

ATTACH MENU/
PLACECARD HERE

USE THESE PAGES TO STORE
SPECIAL PHOTOGRAPHS, LETTERS,
AND MEMENTOES OF YOUR
WEDDING DAY

WHEN YOU'RE BACK HOME

★ Get on with your thank-you letters if you didn't do them before the day.

★ Make sure all rented formalwear was returned and see to outstanding bills.

★ Clean and store the bride's dress.

★ If the bride wants to change her name on bank accounts and so on but hasn't yet done so, she should do it now.

AFTER THE WEDDING, WE MUST REMEMBER TO…

_____

_____

_____

_____

_____

_____

_____

_____

_____

_____

_____

_____

_____

_____

_____

_____

_____

_____

_____

_____

_____

_____

_____

OUR FAVORITE MOMENTS OF OUR WEDDING DAY

First published in the
United Kingdom in 2006 by
Ryland Peters & Small
20–21 Jockey's Fields
London WC1R 4BW
www.rylandpeters.com

and in the United States by
Ryland Peters & Small, Inc.
519 Broadway, 5th Floor
New York, NY 10012

Text by Antonia Swinson
Text, design, and photographs copyright
© Ryland Peters & Small 2006
10 9 8 7 6 5 4 3

ISBN-13: 978-1-84597-284-4
Printed in China

PHOTOGRAPHY CREDITS:
All photographs by Polly Wreford unless otherwise stated.
Key: a=above, b=below, r=right, l=left, c=center.

Craig Fordham Front jacket, pages 15bl, 16al, 17, 18, 22, 39, 40, 45, 78,
113, 114, 115, 116c, 118 both, 120, 123, 141br, 141bcr
Dan Duchars Pages 30ar, 116r, 141al, 141acr, 141br
Sandra Lane Pages 12al, 12bl, 48l, 53 both, 90c
Claire Richardson Pages 10l, 11r, 12bcr, 57, 74l
Carolyn Barber Pages 70, 82l, 87c
Jan Baldwin Pages 49r, 73 all
Chris Everard Pages 12acr, 74r
Tom Leighton Pages 5, 6
Caroline Arber Page 30acr
Christopher Drake Page 37
Daniel Farmer Page 9 inset left
William Lingwood Back jacket